# NEW
# AMERICAN
# INTERIORS

## Innovations in Interior Residential Design

# NEW
# AMERICAN INTERIORS

## Innovations in Interior Residential Design

**Edited by**
**JAMES GRAYSON TRULOVE**

**Whitney Library of Design**
**an imprint of**
**Watson-Guptill Publications/New York**

**HALF-TITLE PAGE:** *Flatiron Loft, Janson Goldstein*
*Photography: Paul Warchol.*
**TITLE PAGE:** *Penthouse Loft, Rogers Marvel*
*Photography: Paul Warchol.*

Project Editor: Holly Jennings
Production Manager: Rebecca Cremonese
Researcher: Neill Heath

First published in 2004 by Whitney Library of Design,
an imprint of Watson-Guptill Publications, a division of
VNU Business Media Inc., 770 Broadway, New York, NY 10003
www.watsonguptill.com

**Library of Congress Control Number:** 2004107318

ISBN: 0-8230-3177-2

Manufactured in China

First Printing, 2004

1 2 3 4 5 6 7 8 9 / 12 11 10 09 08 07 06 05 04

# Contents

# Foreword

In a shift from the previous volumes in the *New American* series—which, except for one on residential gardens, have focused on architecture—this edition takes interior design as its central theme, although architecture is, of course, still an important component. The interiors featured are by both architects and interior designers who, in some cases, work collaboratively and at other times independently. The projects represent a broad range of contemporary interior design and, in the end, provide no concrete evidence of any particular or dominating style or trend. Some of the residences have a comfortable, lived-in quality while others, such as the Lee Residence, a collaboration between Joel Sanders, an architect, and Andy Goldsborough, an interior designer, are celebrations of a minimalist aesthetic.

Renovations of existing apartments are a staple of interior design—every time an apartment changes hands, the new owner has an entirely different vision of how it should look and function, from a live/work space, to a pad for entertaining, to a retreat from the hard-driving urban environment. In many cases, a simple remodeling of an existing space is not enough. The client (often the owner/designer) may insist on a unified design, from the exterior to the interior—in other words, a new house. A client may wish every detail—every dish and every piece of furniture, the placement of every window and door—to be a carefully considered element of the final creation. They may even request that furniture be designed for a specific location and that fabric and paints be made custom.

Whatever the circumstances, it is clear from the broad range of projects in *New American Interiors*, that creating good, memorable interior design is a lot more than just carefully arranged furniture surrounded by coordinated paints, fabrics, and objets d'art. A good design is also dependent upon the ability of the designer or the architect to invent a new visual language for each project that reflects the client's needs and interests and that distinguishes it from other interiors, even though they may share similar elements such as furniture, paint, and fabric. To better understand this, two or more projects by the same interior designer or architect are often featured in this book, allowing the reader to compare a designer's "signature style," apparent in all the work, with the often subtle differences that make each project unique.

**OPPOSITE:** *Vertical House, Lorcan O'Herlihy Architects.*
*Photography: Michael Weschler*
**RIGHT:** *Lee Residence, Andy Goldsborough (Interior Designer) and Joel Sanders (Architect).*
*Photography: Peter Aaron/Esto*

# Beach House

BONETTI/KOZERSKI STUDIO

*Owner:* Withheld
*Interior Design:* Bonetti Kozerski Studio, New York, NY
*Design Team:* Enrico Bonetti and Dominic Kozerski (partners), and Ann Hossler (project architect)
*Photography:* Paul Warchol

*Location:* East Hampton, NY
*Program:* A three-story, renovated beach house with a large spa and yoga studio on the first level; a living room, dining room, kitchen, and outdoor living room on a covered deck on the second level; a master bedroom with bath on the third level; and a roof deck
*Square Footage:* 4000
*Mechanical System:* Forced air
*Major Interior Materials:* Antique oak floors bleached twice then stained with custom-mixed ivory stain; spa floors and wet areas are tumbled Jerusalem limestone; decks are seasoned solid cedar; and ivory, polished, Venetian plaster walls
*Furnishings:* Custom furniture (sofas, low dining table and chairs, bed, outdoor dining table and benches, console tables) is made of solid reclaimed Indonesian swamp teak with a burnished wax finish and is designed by Bonetti/Kozerski Studio; carved chair by Nathaniel Gluska; and antique Asian artifacts
*Fixtures:* Kohler
*Appliances and Equipment:* Miele, Viking, and Sub-Zero

## Design

Adjacent to a larger property, the house was conceived of as a retreat that is used for guests and large family gatherings. A raised walkway connects the two houses across a bank of trees. The main ground-floor room opens out directly onto the pool deck, which provides some shelter from the sun and a place to lounge. A simple tent, similar in design to the upper outdoor "living room" tent on the deck above, provides sun protection over the outdoor dining area. Flanking the pool on the other side of the deck are two large outdoor futon beds on custom-designed cedar bases. After passing through the pool deck lounge, two sliding doors off a small lobby lead to either the yoga room or spa. The two rooms are separated with sliding screens (of natural pineapple cloth with a gauze interlayer) that obscure the view into the spa but allow the sunlight to penetrate into the space. The floor and wall material changes to Jerusalem limestone. A large sunken tub overlooks the waterfall garden. An open stair leads to the second-floor dining area with a view over the bluff at the end of the garden to the bay. A low dining table and chairs provide an unobstructed view. The dining table is made of a solid, single piece of reclaimed teak. The low chairs allow for an Asian-style dining experience combined with

**RIGHT:** *Living area*

Western-style comfort. A large double-sided fireplace separates the dining space from the living room. The large L-shaped sofa has a solid teak platform and deep futons filled with natural cotton and covered with soft, washed, natural linen. There is also a solid carved wood chair by Swiss artist Nathaniel Gluska. A long, wood, low console table with custom-made storage baskets and wood boxes is situated behind the sofa. This same console design becomes a serving credenza in the dining room.

From the open kitchen, double sliding doors open to the outdoor living room, an elevated deck space overlooking the garden and pool areas. Seating on this deck/living space is provided by a series of cedar platforms that are on casters and can be arranged in several different configurations. Outdoor cushions and pillows are arranged on the platforms while other platforms are left bare and are used as dining and working surfaces. The master bedroom suite is on the top floor, up the open stairs from the internal living room. The bed floats on a natural, solid teak platform facing the bay. On either side of the bed are custom-designed bedside tables. A fireplace on one side creates a small space for quiet reading while an external balcony allows commanding views over the entire bay.

First Floor Plan

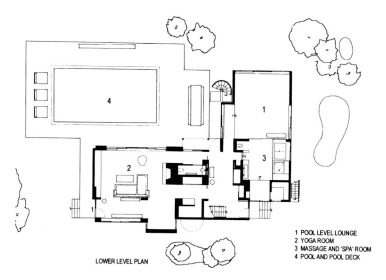

1 POOL LEVEL LOUNGE
2 YOGA ROOM
3 MASSAGE AND 'SPA' ROOM
4 POOL AND POOL DECK

LOWER LEVEL PLAN

Second Floor Plan

5 LIVING ROOM
6 DINING ROOM
7 KITCHEN
8 OUTDOOR LIVING

INTERMEDIATE LEVEL PLAN

Third Floor Plan

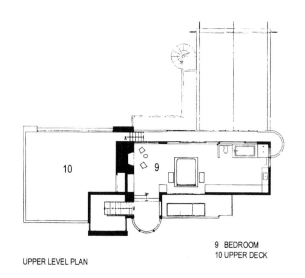

9 BEDROOM
10 UPPER DECK

UPPER LEVEL PLAN

**LEFT AND ABOVE:** *Dining area with custom furniture by Bonetti/Kozerski Studio*
**FOLLOWING PAGES:** *Master bedroom*

# Chun Residence

## BUSH INTERIORS

*Owners:* Han Jin and Yoon Hee Chun
*Interior Design:* Bush Interiors, Marina Del Rey, CA
*Architect:* Chun Studio, Marina Del Rey, CA
*Engineer:* Jon Brody Consulting Engineers
*General Contractor:* Minardos Construction
*Photography:* Tim Street-Porter

*Location:* Santa Monica, CA
*Program:* New construction consisting of an entry, living room, dining room, open kitchen, breakfast area, den, master bedroom and bath suite, three bedrooms, three bathrooms, and a garage
*Square Footage:* 5000
*Structural System:* Steel, wood frame, and poured-in-place concrete
*Major Exterior Finishes:* Redwood siding and decks, steel, glass, and concrete
*Major Interior Materials:* Cherry paneling, maple and slate floors, glass, and concrete
*Furnishings and Storage:* Eurotech Construction
*Doors and Hardware:* Forms and Surfaces, Spectrum Oaks, and D-Line
*Appliances and Equipment:* Sub-Zero, Thermador, and Fisher & Paykel

### Design

The interiors were designed to be in harmony with the architecture. The furnishings that were selected are modern in form and material and complement the Asian sensibility used thoughout the house.

As in traditional Asian design, organic shapes and materials were introduced to contrast and highlight the rectilinear volumes of the building. This is best illustrated in Hans Wegner's hoop chair in the living room, the Italian bent rattan loop chairs in the master bedroom, and the Danish chairs used in both the dining room and breakfast areas.

Color was used strategically to pick up tones from the architecture. In the den, dark gray carpeting, woods, and upholstered pieces match the existing concrete hearth. The orange ottomans reference the color of the Douglas fir ceiling and add life to the room.

Color was also used as a tool to take the eye back and forth between the interior and exterior spaces. Oranges and pinks were chosen for the game room not only to create visual energy, but also to be easily seen when outside on the upper deck furnishings.

**RIGHT:** *Living room*

Second Floor Plan

First Floor Plan

**ABOVE:** *Stairway to second floor*
**OPPOSITE:** *Upper deck*

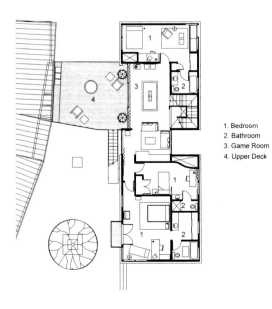

1. Bedroom
2. Bathroom
3. Game Room
4. Upper Deck

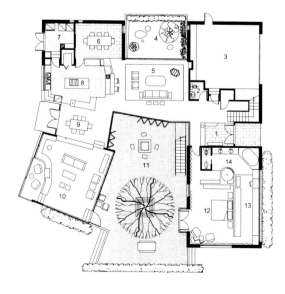

1. Entry
2. Powder Room
3. Garage
4. Zen Garden
5. Living
6. Dining
7. Laundry
8. Kitchen
9. Breakfast
10. Den
11. Center Deck
12. Master Bedroom
13. Master Closet
14. Master Bathroom

**OPPOSITE:** *Dining room*
**THIS PAGE:** *Kitchen*

**ABOVE:** *Game room*
**OPPOSITE:** *Master bedroom*

# Berkeley Bungalow

## DAVIDS KILLORY ARCHITECTS

*Owner:* Withheld
*Architect:* Davids Killory Architects, Berkeley, CA
*Design Team:* Rene Davids and Christine Killory
*Engineers:* Hohbach Lewin, Michael Ross (structural)
*General Contractor:* Alward Construction, Inc.
*Consultant:* Jensen Van Lienden (geotechnical)
*Landscape Contractor:* Lazar Landscape
*Photography:* Marion Brenner, Dana Buntrock, Leroy
Howard, and Davids Killory Architects

*Location:* Berkeley, CA
*Program:* Remodeling an existing three-story single family
house with five bedrooms, three bathrooms, a shower room,
open living space, library, office, decks, a porch and bridge,
and carport
*Square Footage:* 3300
*Mechanical System:* Forced air
*Major Exterior Materials:* Integrated color plaster, clear
anodized aluminum bar grating, Ipe hardwood, aluminum
bridge and stair, stainless steel handrail, tubular steel columns,
and clear anodized aluminum siding
*Major Interior Materials:* Black slate, stainless steel, white
laminated glass, melamine-impregnated birch plywood, red-
oak flooring stained black, woven stainless-steel mesh, stain-
less steel handrail, Trusjoist ceiling truss joists, Panellite,
Lumasite, soapstone, Bendheim titanium, and mirror glass
*Furnishings:* Custom cabinetry and metalwork designed by
the architect, various furniture by B&B Italia, Knoll, Alivar,
Design Within Reach, and IKEA
*Doors and Hardware:* Bonelli (clear anodized aluminum
frame windows) and Haefele (hardware)
*Fixtures:* Dornbracht, Sunrise Speciality, Waterworks,
Porcher, and Keramag
*Appliances and Equipment:* Thermador, Sub-Zero, Miele,
Viking, Maytag, and Ventahood

## Design

The house is organized on three levels. To mitigate the
extraordinary view, visual and spatial connections
between the main living spaces and the more intimate
areas on the periphery are emphasized, as are connections between the front and backyard landscapes. On the
west facade, the house is wrapped by an aluminum
screen enclosing porches and decks.

The original intention was to make a spinelike bridge
that would pass up the hill from the street, go directly
through the house and finally land on the hill behind it,
but local zoning laws dictated a series of directional
shifts. Since the bridge creates a link from the street up
to the front door, moves through the public and private

**RIGHT:** *Living, dining, and
kitchen areas*

spaces of the house and ends on the hill, it becomes a dynamic element in a context of continuous flowing space. As the bridge moves through the house, it connects its upper and lower levels to the landscape, mediating between inside and out.

With less distinction between public and private in contemporary life, fewer rooms are required to establish degrees of social intimacy. Food preparation, dining, and socializing all share the same open space, modulated by shifts in ceiling height and furniture placement. A sliding stainless-steel panel divides the third floor living space. Water elements on all three floors are dispersed around the perimeter. Materials and finishes are classic white walls, hardwood floors stained black, polished black slate, matte gray soapstone, translucent glass, and honed stainless steel.

**RIGHT:** *View on to deck*
**OPPOSITE:** *View of two story-living area*
**BOTTOM:** *View from second-floor balcony*

Model of House

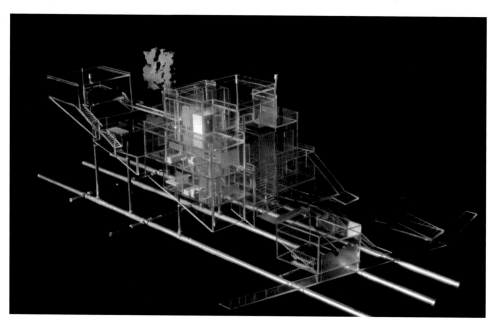

**LEFT AND ABOVE:** *Master bathroom*
**FAR LEFT:** *Kitchen*

# Stretch Residence

## E. COBB ARCHITECTS

**Owners:** Aidan and Elizabeth Stretch
**Architect:** E. Cobb Architects, Seattle, WA
**Design Team:** Eric Cobb (principal), Ian Butcher (job captain), and Sharyn Atkins
**Interior Design:** Elizabeth Stretch, Stretch Design
**Engineer:** James Harriott, Harriott Engineers, Inc. (structural)
**General Contractor:** David Rohrer, Constantly Building
**Photography:** Paul Warchol

**Location:** Seattle, WA
**Program:** A primary residence for a young family
**Square Footage:** 3000
**Major Exterior Materials:** Vertical T&G cedar siding and painted fiber-cement board
**Major Interior Materials:** Maple hardwood flooring, maple cabinetry, granite tile, blackened steel fireplace surround, and painted structural steel
**Furnishings and Storage:** Christian (sofa), Italinteriors (armchair), Henry Built (dining table), Herman Miller (dining chairs), B&B Italia (side tables), Driscol Robbins (rugs), and Urban Ease (Poliform bar stools)
**Fixtures:** Kohler, Toto, Arwa, Juno, Rab, Columbia, and Prescolite
**Appliances and Equipment:** Sub-Zero, Wolf, Thermador, and Bosch

### Design

The Stretch House is located on the west-facing slope of Queen Anne Hill in Seattle. With a modest construction budget, a hybrid structure was conceived to utilize selected assets of an existing structure (foundation, garage, some wall framing). The new construction is a two-story structure that takes full advantage of light exposure and Puget Sound views.

The design of the house groups and separates spaces of different scales and relationships. Through careful planning with the owner, selected smaller, domestic-scaled spaces—bathrooms, bedrooms, closets, a laundry room, playroom, and home office—are tightly programmed along a simple hall on the first floor.

The second floor is configured primarily from site conditions. Zoning setbacks allowed for a six-foot front yard cantilever. The higher floor elevation offers spectacular views to the west and southwest with a wall along the southwest to block views of adjacent neighbors. The result is a singular loft space, loosely fitted for flexible use. This large space is placed above the domestic floor, but not "fitted" to the lower dimensions. The architecture of this piece is defined by simple, abstract

**RIGHT:** *Living room*

surfaces and floor-to-ceiling glass. Specific living areas are created within the loft space by the placement of furniture and other objects.

The interior material palette is singular, allowing the scale of space to be the primary differentiating condition throughout the house. A single stone is used in all of the wet areas. All dry floors are maple hardwood and walls and ceilings are painted white. The same closet door detailing repeats throughout the house. The architecture and interiors are intentionally restrained and spare.

Second Floor Plan

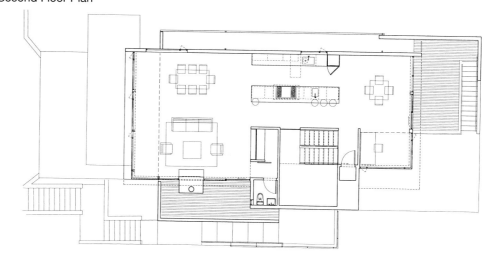

First Floor Plan

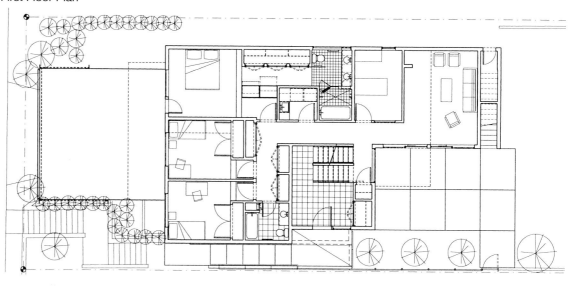

**LEFT:** *South elevation*
**OPPOSITE, LEFT:** *East elevation*
**OPPOSITE, RIGHT:** *View to west at sunset*

**OPPOSITE:** *Living room*
**ABOVE:** *Kitchen*
**RIGHT:** *View of dining area from kitchen*

# Franck-Triem Residence

FT ARCHITECTURE + DESIGN

*Owners:* Peter Franck and Kathleen Triem
*Architect:* FT Architecture + Design, Ghent, NY
*Design Team:* Peter Franck and Kathleen Triem (principals)
*General Contractor:* FT Architecture + Design (construction management)
*Consultant:* Filament 33 (lighting)
*Photography:* Bärbel Miebach

*Location:* Ghent, NY
*Program:* New construction consisting of two children's bedrooms, a living/dining/kitchen loft space, master bedroom, three baths, reading room, outdoor terraces, a gallery/painting studio, and workshop
*Square Footage:* 3000
*Structural System:* Slab on grade, LVL wood joists, and steel frame
*Mechanical System:* Radiant heat
*Major Exterior Materials:* Alcove bluestone and copper
*Major Interior Materials:* Terrazzo tile (flooring), concrete, carpet, and Sheetrock
*Furnishings and Storage:* Wood side chairs, acrylic coffee table, flea market chaise lounge reupholstered by the architects, and sofa by M2L
*Doors and Hardware:* Loewen (exterior doors) and Omnia (interior hardware)
*Appliances and Equipment:* Viking, Amana, and Thermador

## Design

The site is a hilltop field in New York's Hudson Valley and is adjacent to a contemporary sculpture park that the architects curate. The design of this home, therefore, is meant to explore the boundaries of art practices and architecture. Influenced by sculptor Richard Serra's earlier projects that investigate the manner in which rational objects can create a datum against the landscape, the form of the house is conceived as a minimalist object set into the landscape. It projects the strength and clarity of an isolated prime object, yet there is, simultaneously, a complex and dynamic relationship with the earth.

The composition of the building is an irregular trapezoid and the mass is chamfered in sympathy with the sloping site. The house slices into the grade and the resultant connection with the land creates a variety of spatial connections with the interior of the house, although one must continuously encircle the site and explore the interiors to get a sense of the whole. Each interior space and each facade have entirely different relationships to the view of the Catskill Mountains and to the ground plane.

To capitalize on the views, the main loft space, containing the living, dining, and kitchen areas, is located

**ABOVE:** *Dining area*
**OPPOSITE:** *Living area*

upstairs. The master bedroom is also on the upper level, but at the rear of the house, which has a private eastern exposure to a wooded hill beyond. Two ramps connect the upstairs living area to the sloping site. Downstairs, the entry gallery and the library open onto French stone patios.

The exterior materials are the color of the earth. Local alcove bluestone creates a heavy, textured base for the object and ties it to the ground. The upper section of the house is copper, its crisp lines provide a contrast with the irregular masonry and the precise fabrication of the seams emphasize the horizontal quality of the mass. The copper attained a dark bronze patina immediately upon installation. It continually changes in perception according to different lighting conditions and is in close harmony with the stone.

While the exterior has a natural feel, the interior is meant to be crisp, clean, and modern. The major living space is inspired by the prototypical New York artist's loft with a large open space for living, dining, and cooking. It has white terrazzo tile and custom glossy-white cabinet doors over Home Depot cabinets, which provides a luxurious finish at an affordable cost.

**RIGHT:** *Entry ramp*

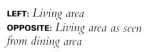

**LEFT AND ABOVE:** *Stairway from living area to upper-level master bedroom*

**OPPOSITE AND ABOVE:** *Master bedroom*
**ABOVE, RIGHT:** *View to bedroom from hallway*

**ABOVE:** *Veiw of the ramps and terrace*
**OPPOSITE:** *Shorter ramp connects the porch to the living space*

# Lee Residence

JOEL SANDERS ARCHITECT
ANDY GOLDSBOROUGH INTERIOR DESIGN

*Owner:* Withheld
*Architect:* Joel Sanders Architect, New York, NY
*Interior Design:* Andy Goldsborough Interior Design,
New York, NY
*Engineer:* Jack Green Associates
*General Contractor:* Foundations, Saif Sumaida
*Consultants:* Lighting Collaborative, Lewis Herman
(lighting)
*Photography:* Peter Aaron/Esto

*Location:* New York, NY
*Program:* Complete renovation of an existing apartment to
include an open floor plan with a dance-practice area, two
convertible sleeping spaces for guests, a study, master suite,
kitchen, living, and dining areas
*Square Footage:* 1850
*Major Interior Materials:* Epoxy (floors, walls, ceilings),
brushed, powder-coated, quarter-sawn oak (cabinets, floors),
Corian, and glass
*Fixtures:* Duravit and Dornbracht

## Design

This design was based on the idea of a central
core that would contain most of the storage and the
bathrooms, and that would provide circulation through
the apartment while leaving the south and east window
walls free for maximum admission of light into primary
living areas. Custom moldings were made so that the
floor, wall, and ceiling planes could be seamlessly poured
in an epoxy resin material emphasizing the flowing
nature of the apartment. Custom built-in furniture
incorporates existing columns in the living room/dining
room; in the master bedroom a built-in platform bed
seems to fold down from the wall plane.

The color palette consists of pale, watery-green colors
that provide a soothing backdrop from the busy
cityscape. Vibrant red is used for the leather on the bio-
morphic adjustable lounge chair in the living room and
for the silk headboard in the master bedroom. This color
complements the primarily green setting and gives the
apartment an Asian-inspired feeling. Acid-etched glass
and mirrors on many of the vertical surfaces in the
apartment give the illusion of a higher ceiling and add
dimension to the wall planes.

The overall focus of the apartment was on material
exploration and contrast between matte and very
glossy reflective surfaces. The shiny epoxy material was

**RIGHT:** *Living area*

used primarily in the wet areas and in the recessed master bedroom alcove. Bleached oak was used for all of the custom kitchen cabinetry and the flooring that circulates around the core of the space, which is separated by an aluminum strip. In the master bedroom the linear tufting of the Eames desk chair is repeated in the custom bed cover, further emphasizing the bending and folding of vertical and horizontal surfaces.

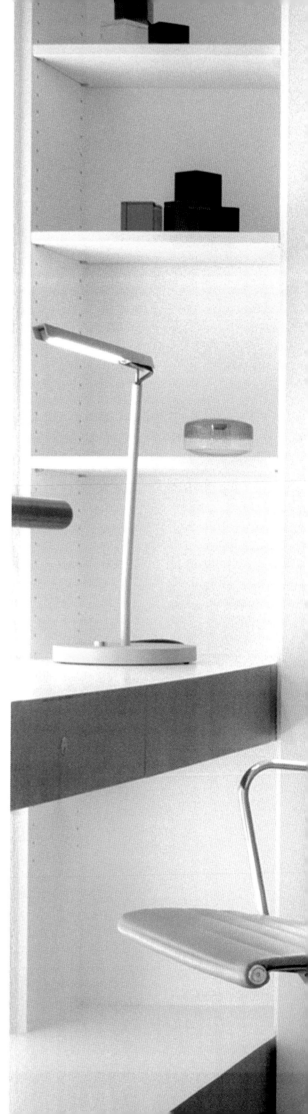

**RIGHT:** *The study*

**LEFT, ABOVE, AND OPPOSITE:**
*Views of master bathtub and shower*
**FOLLOWING PAGES:** *Panoramic view of dance-practice area that doubles as guest room and study*

# Fitch O'Rourke Residence

ROBERT M. GURNEY, ARCHITECT

*Owners:* Mary C. Fitch and Ron O'Rourke
*Architect:* Robert M. Gurney, Architect, Washington, DC
*Design Team:* Robert M. Gurney and Hito Martinez
(project designers)
*Engineers:* Tony Beale, Advance Engineers (structural), and
Brian Ford (mechanical)
*Interior Design:* Therese Baron Gurney
*Photography:* Paul Warchol and Hoachlander Davis
Photography

*Location:* Washington, DC
*Program:* For this complete renovation of an existing townhouse, the client requested a two-bedroom, two-study residence on the upper three levels, and a one-bedroom rental
unit in the basement.
*Square Footage:* 4400
*Mechanical System:* Heat pump and forced air
*Major Interior Materials:* Board-formed concrete, steel
(force-rusted, stainless, perforated, painted), block aluminum,
lead-coated copper, copper wire cloth, Uniclad corrugated
panels, clear and sandblasted glass, Kalwall and Lumicite
translucent panels, limestone tile, Kirkstone and limestone
countertops, maple and mahogany veneer cabinets and wall
panels, and maple and Brazilian cherry flooring
*Furnishings and Storage:* Burgers' Cabinet Shop
*Doors and Hardware:* A&S Window Associates, Northeast
Ironworks, and Modric (locksets)
*Windows:* Weathershield (wooden windows), A&S Window
Associates (steel), Kalwall (curtain wall), and Maryland
International Glass (custom)
*Fixtures:* Lightolier, Extiluz, Stonco, and Lutron
*Appliances and Equipment:* Viking and Sub-Zero

## Design

The renovation, which began with two brick side walls
and a dirt-floor basement, amounted to building a new
house inside an old shell. The project faced three major
constraints: a long, narrow footprint (sixty-three-feet-
long, seventeen-feet-wide on the front, narrowing to
thirteen feet); the property's location in a historic district requiring the front facade to be kept intact; and the
client's limited budget.

The design for the house transcends the building's narrow confines by combining a traditional orthogonal
scheme with a curving geometry. The resulting arrangement creates dramatic spaces and levels throughout the
house. To accentuate light, the living room takes advantage of the house's southern exposure and the new rear
facade brings much needed light into the inner quarters
of the house. Building and finishing materials were chosen to create a varied and warm mix of colors and textures to admit and modulate light.

**RIGHT:** *Living area*

Basement Floor Plan

First Floor Plan

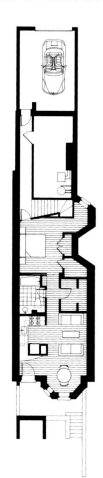

Axonometric

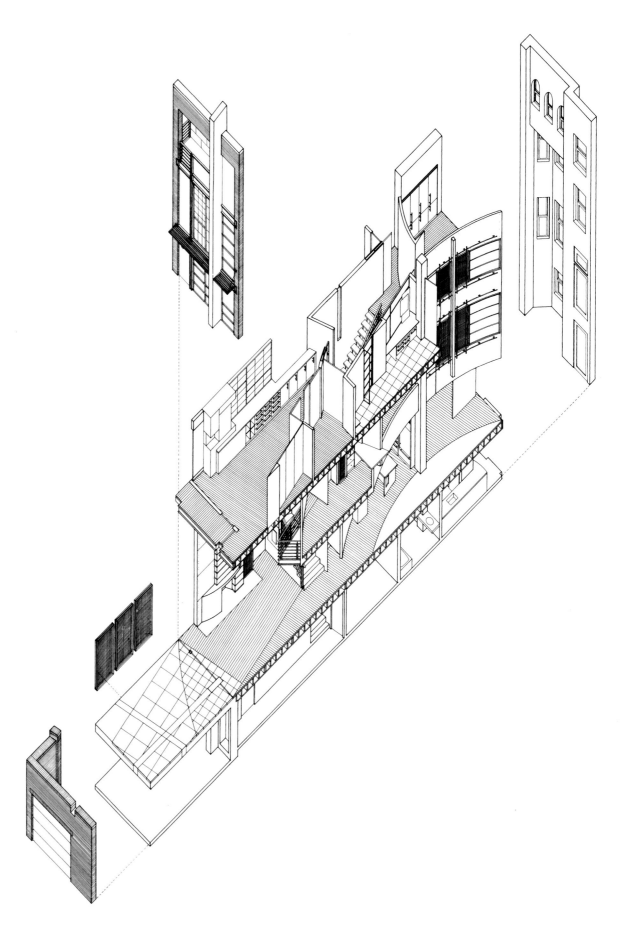

Second Floor Plan

Third Floor Plan

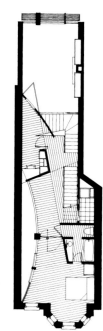

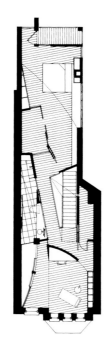

**ABOVE:** *Renovated rear facade*
**RIGHT:** *View of entry from second floor balcony*

**ABOVE:** *Dining area*
**OPPOSITE:** *Kitchen*

**OPPOSITE:** *View to first floor*
**ABOVE, LEFT:** *Third-floor skylight*
**ABOVE, RIGHT:** *Second-floor corridor*

**ABOVE:** *Master bedroom*

**ABOVE, LEFT:** *Master bathroom*
**ABOVE, RIGHT:** *Bathroom*
**FOLLOWING PAGES:** *View of terrace from living area; view of living area from terrace*

# Perry Street Loft

## HARIRI & HARIRI ARCHITECTURE

*Owner:* Michael Aram
*Architect:* Hariri & Hariri Architecture, New York, NY
*Design Team:* Gisue Hariri, Mojgan Hariri, Thierry Pfister, and Mason White
*Engineers:* Robert Silman & Associates (structural) and Szekely Engineering (mechanical)
*General Contractor:* Fountainhead Construction
*Photography:* Paul Warchol

*Location:* New York, NY
*Program:* Renovation of a two-story loft apartment to create an open plan consisting of a living room, dining room, kitchen, master suite, and guest bedrooms
*Square Footage:* 1715
*Structural System:* Steel post and beam, wood joists
*Major Interior Materials:* Drywall, stucco, fiberglass, concrete, and wood
*Furnishings and Storage:* Custom designed by the owner
*Doors and Hardware:* Solid wood painted, Schlage, and Stanley (hardware)
*Fixtures:* Kroin and Kohler
*Appliances and Equipment:* GE, Sub-Zero, and KitchenAide

### Design

This project was driven by a desire to create a temple for art, a sanctuary for the soul, and a refuge for the body in a dense, noisy urban environment.

Architecturally, the loft is organized around light, bringing in as much natural and artificial light into the loft as possible. Entering the apartment on the upper level, visitors are greeted by a two-story light wall embedded with fluorescent tubes. The wall serves as a vertical connector between the two floors of the loft, organizing the space and circulation while providing soothing illumination. The space on both floors runs from the street to the garden, allowing natural light to penetrate and filter throughout the loft. The kitchen and bathrooms are along the east wall behind translucent screens on tracks. These screens conceal the spaces behind them and provide privacy while allowing natural light to enter.

At the rear of the loft, overlooking the garden, is a double-story living room enclosed by a glass curtain wall. A shallow trough of water stretches from the living room out to the garden where it culminates in a fountain, uniting the interior and exterior. The fountain is a piece of carved marble from the Moghul period.

**RIGHT:** *View of living area and light well adjacent to stairs*

First Floor Plan

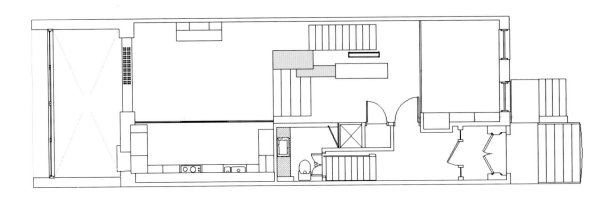

Ground Floor Plan

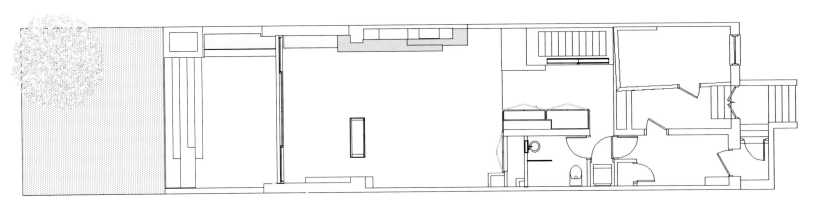

Section

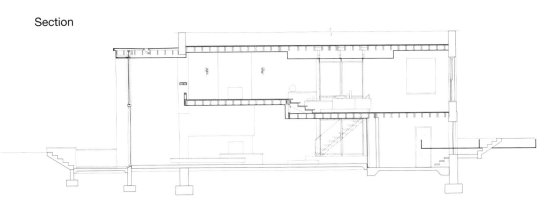

**BELOW:** *Stair detail*
**OPPOSITE:** *View of light well at entry level*

**OPPOSITE:** *View of dining room*
**RIGHT:** *Kitchen detail*
**BOTTOM LEFT:** *View of kitchen open* .
**BOTTOM RIGHT:** *View of kitchen closed*

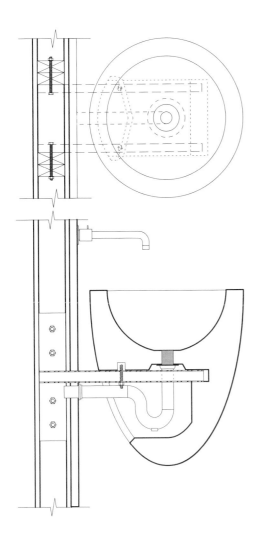

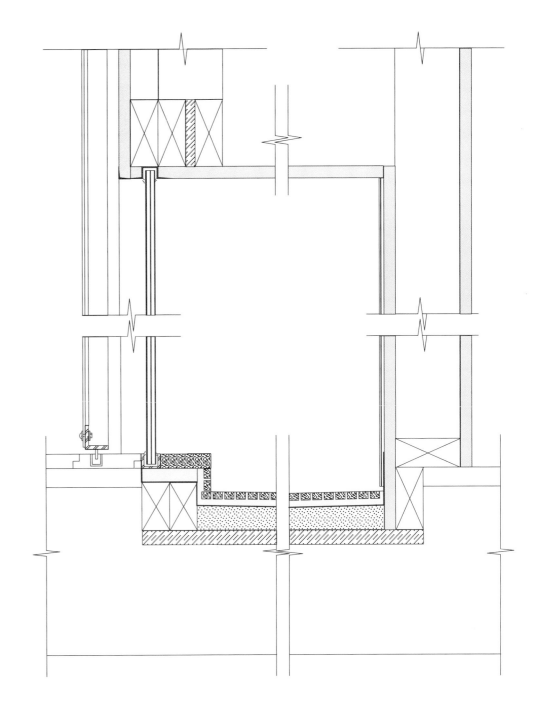

**OPPOSITE:** *Bathroom vanity*
**ABOVE AND RIGHT:** *Lavatory details*
**TOP RIGHT AND FAR RIGHT:** *Shower detail*

# Park Avenue Apartment

## JANSON GOLDSTEIN

*Owner:* Withheld
*Interior Design:* Janson Goldstein, New York, NY
*Design Team:* Hal Goldstein and Mark Janson (principals),
Paola Rosales (project architect)
*Engineer:* MEP Engineer (power engineering)
*General Contractor:* Silverlining
*Consultants:* Bill Jansing (lighting design) and Donald
Kaufman (color)
*Photography:* Michael Weschler

*Location:* New York, NY
*Program:* Renovation of an existing apartment that includes
an entry/gallery space, formal living room, library/video
room, formal dining room, informal loft space juxtaposed to
kitchen, and four bedrooms
*Square Footage:* 4000
*Major Interior Materials:* Wood flooring (I. J. Peiser), plaster
(Art-in-Construction), and travertine
*Furnishings and Storage:* Jean Michel Frank (sofas), Alison
Berger (chandeliers), and Janson Goldstein (leather and teak table)
*Appliances and Equipment:* Viking and Sub-Zero

### Design

The public area of the apartment is designed as a free-
flowing spatial experience that is conducive to the
owners' lifestyle and viewing of their extensive collection of art and objects. Within the fluidity of the plan,
many rooms have their own identity. The entry/gallery
space connects the living and dining areas and features
photographs by Roni Horn and custom-designed glass
chandeliers by Alison Berger. The formal living room
features sofas by Jean Michel Frank, French modern slip
chairs, and a custom-designed leather and teak table by
Janson Goldstein. Two slabs of travertine are used to create the fireplace surround and provide a backdrop for
freestanding objects such as glasswork and pottery.
Adjoining the living room is the library, with a silk-and-
wool area rug over a cork floor. Custom metal shelving
displays both books and small art work. A large Christo
is featured in this space, located over a custom-designed
sofa. Chairs are by Eero Saarinen and Hans Wegner.

The private areas are designed for comfort and warmth
around their own unique color. A deep plum color sets
up a Japanese motif in the master suite. Lime green and
blue work with mid-century modern pieces by George
Nelson and fabrics by Charles and Ray Eames in the
children's rooms.

**RIGHT:** *Living room with slabs
of travertine creating fireplace
surround*

Floor Plan

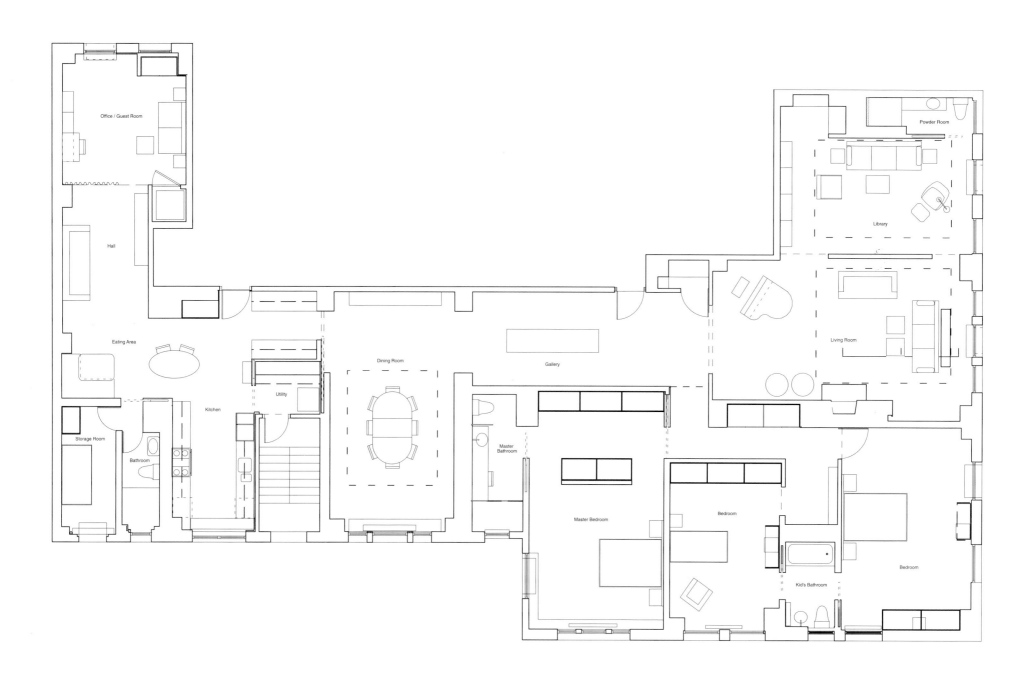

Office / Guest Room

Powder Room

Library

Hall

Living Room

Eating Area

Dining Room

Gallery

Utility

Kitchen

Storage Room

Master Bathroom

Bathroom

Master Bedroom

Bedroom

Bedroom

Kid's Bathroom

**LEFT:** *Kitchen*
**ABOVE:** *Master bedroom*
**RIGHT:** *Master bathroom*

# Penthouse Loft

## ROGERS MARVEL ARCHITECTS

*Owner:* Withheld
*Architect:* Rogers Marvel Architects, New York, NY
*Design Team:* Rob Rogers and Jonathan Marvel (partners-in-charge), Alissa Bucher (project architect), Mark Nye, Emma Morris, Mike Jacobs, Aaron Young, Eugene Colberg (project team), and Alexandr Neratoff (architect of record)
*Engineers:* Ross Dalland (structural) and P. A. Collins (mechanical, electrical, plumbing)
*General Contractor:* James Lee Construction
*Consultants:* Dirtworks/David Kamp, Lara Normand (landscape), Arc Light Design (lighting), Cerami and Associates, Inc. (acoustics), and R. A. Heintges Architects and Consultants (glazing and skylights)
*Photography:* Paul Warchol

*Location:* New York, NY
*Program:* Renovation of an existing industrial loft with the addition of a new penthouse and roof terrace
*Square Footage:* 6800 (interior), 3350 (terraces)
*Structural System:* Existing masonry building with cast-iron interior columns, steel beams, and concrete floor slabs
*Furnishings and Storage:* Wood cabinets (custom by James Lee Construction), painted steel cabinets (Forster by 3-D Lab), furniture and lighting from the owner's collection, and ICON Interiors (window treatments)
*Doors and Hardware:* Megawood, Omnia, Stanley, Rixson, and Colonial
*Windows:* Mahogany with aluminum exterior cladding, triple glazed for acoustical performance (Megawood)
*Lighting:* Lightolier (downlights), LiteLab (art lighting), and Lutron Controls

### Design

This apartment combines a gallery and living quarters for an art and textile collector. The design marries two spatial types—the urban interior loft and the modernist/object building. The apartment occupies the sixth floor of an old paper factory, with a new penthouse and roof terrace above. The west facade of the residence is formed by a dramatically angled window providing a view of the Hudson river. Various manipulations of light connect the sixth floor to the penthouse. Light enters the three-level stairwell and filters through glass stair treads. This strip of light continues around the perimeter of the sixth-floor living space. Sculptural skylights reappear throughout the apartment, emerging on the terrace as light-filled objects in fields of tall grasses.

The penthouse has the feeling of a small isolated pavilion. From the roof deck the wide metal eaves effectively erase any notion of what is below, giving a view only of the Hudson river and nearby rooftops.

**RIGHT:** *Penthouse living area*

Main Floor Plan

Penthouse Floor Plan

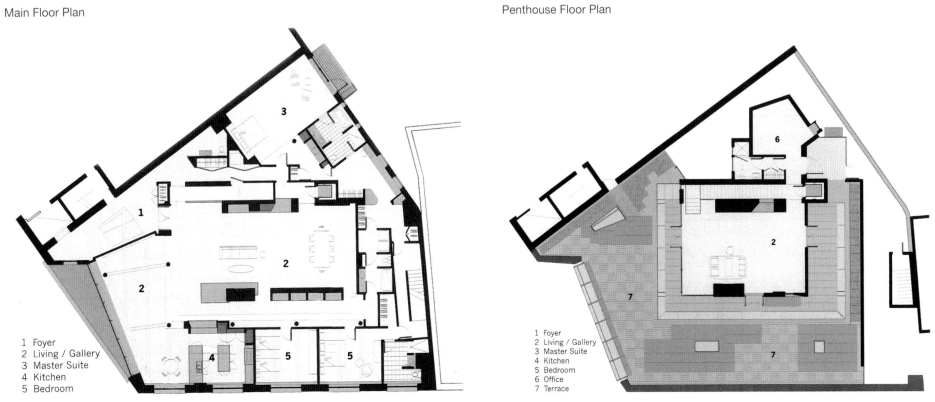

1 Foyer
2 Living / Gallery
3 Master Suite
4 Kitchen
5 Bedroom

1 Foyer
2 Living / Gallery
3 Master Suite
4 Kitchen
5 Bedroom
6 Office
7 Terrace

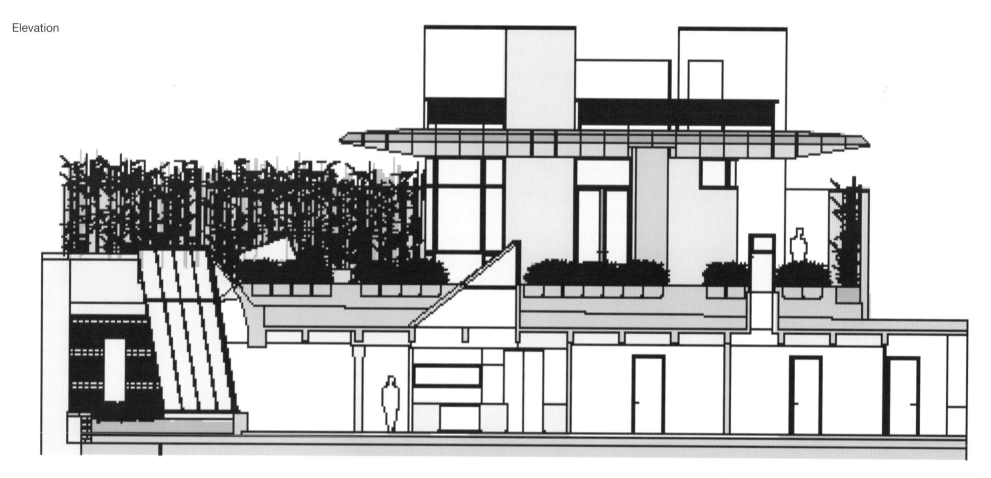

**OPPOSITE AND RIGHT:** *Penthouse terrace*

**FOLLOWING PAGES:** *A series of sculptural skylights appear as lanterns in beach grasses on the main terrace*

THIS SPREAD: *A skylit glass stair leads from gallery to penthouse pavilion and to upper-roof terrace*

**OPPOSITE:** *Kitchen*
**RIGHT AND FOLLOWING PAGES:**
*Living room/gallery*

# Franklin Street Loft

TOCAR, INC.

*Owner:* Withheld
*Interior Design:* Tocar, Inc., New York, NY
*Architect:* Roger Hirsch Architect, New York, NY
*Design Team:* Roger Hirsch and Myriam Corti (architects)
and Susan Bednar and Christina Sulivan (interior designers)
*Photography:* Lisa Keresi, Tocar

*Location:* New York, NY
*Program:* A primary residence allowing for separate spaces
for college-aged children, including four bedrooms, three-
and-one-half baths. The upper two stories are spaces for the
adult couple, the lower two stories for the children.
*Square Footage:* 2000
*Major Interior Materials:* Ebony, handmade ceramic tiles,
and plaster
*Furnishings and Storage:* B&B Italia and custom furniture by
Tocar, Inc.

## Design

For the renovation of this residential loft, the clients
wanted an open design incorporating materials and
details that would complement their extensive collection of contemporary art, photography, and furniture.

A centrally-located ebony wall houses a guest bed
behind flush panels. The bed folds down and translucent
curtains extend to create a private sleeping area for
guests. A floating teak counter transforms into two individual work areas with flip-top desks and drawers
between them. When not in use, the simple counter
helps to frame the large projection TV screen. The guest
bathroom features off-white, handmade tiles from Peru
that are laid horizontally across the wall.

In the modestly sized master bedroom, the length of the
space is exaggerated by the long, flanking passageways
on either side of the room. Hanging clothes are housed
in the freestanding, fully enclosed towers in the dressing
room, which is located behind the bed and set off with
an etched-glass wall. From the bedroom side, hazy
images of the orange dressing room towers glow with
color behind the glass, adding depth to the room.

**RIGHT:** *Living room*

RIGHT: *Entry*
OPPOSITE: *Kitchen*

**ABOVE:** *Dining area with ebony wall*
**OPPOSITE:** *Fold-down bed located on opposite side of ebony wall*

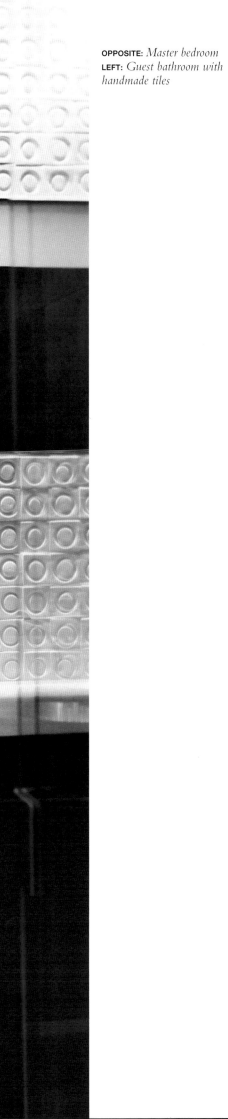

# Central Park West Apartment

JANSON GOLDSTEIN

*Owner:* Withheld
*Interior Design:* Janson Goldstein, New York, NY
*Design Team:* Mark Janson and Hal Goldstein (partners), Paola Rosales (project architect), and Randal Larsen (detailer)
*Engineer:* Tri-Power Engineering
*General Contractor:* Silverlining
*Consultants:* Bill Jansing (lighting design) and Zack Zanoli (art lighting)
*Suppliers:* Silverlining (painting), John Pompea (metal fabrication), Decorative Arts Studio (custom furniture), D. Magnon & Company (terrazzo flooring), I. J. Peiser (wood flooring), Art-in-Construction (plaster), and Fourth Street Studios (custom silk carpet)
*Photography:* Paul Warchol

*Location:* New York, NY
*Program:* Complete renovation of an existing apartment to include a kitchen, living room, dining room, master suite, guest room, and home office
*Square Footage:* 2200
*Major Interior Materials:* Terrazzo, bleached wood, plaster, French limestone, teak, mosaic marble, and Corian
*Furnishings and Storage:* Jean Michel Frank sofa, custom floor lamp by Alison Berger, red leather side chairs by Christian Liagre, Prouvé chair, silk carpet by Fourth Street Studios, and custom side table by Janson Goldstein
*Fixtures:* Kroin and Grohe
*Appliances and Equipment:* GE Profile

## Design

The apartment was designed to display the owner's collections of art, furniture, and objects. With expansive views of New York's Central Park, the project is a home for living, viewing, and exploring the many things within it.

In the public areas a terrazzo floor flows from the entry into the living and dining areas, providing a gallery quality to these spaces. The ceiling plane is manipulated to have a sculpted presence with recessed lighting located for specific art works on the walls. HVAC and window treatments are integrated into the ceiling design.

A bleached wood floor is used for the "private" areas (master suite, library, guest room, bath). At the bed, the wood floor turns up the wall, culminating in a suede headboard that provides both comfort and a reference line for the Uta Barth photographs hanging above. Cantilevered steel side tables completes the composition. Bath areas have a serene feel with limestone floors and teak wood with an oil finish. Plaster walls, which match the limestone floor,

**RIGHT:** *Living room*

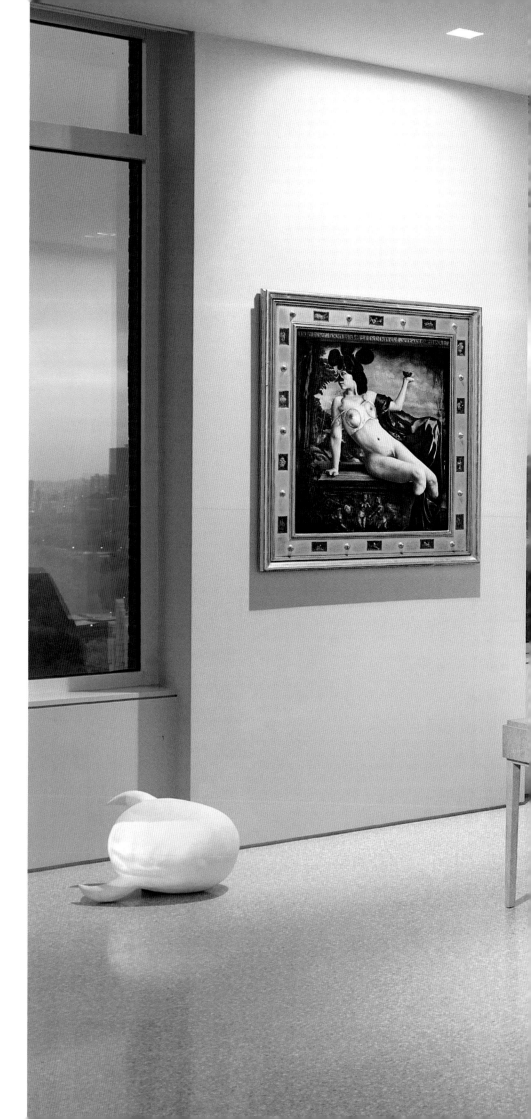

add to the texture of the space and provide a counterbalance to the cool-white mosaic marble and white Corian counter tops.

The interior design is a blend of twentieth-century design with pieces by Jean Nouvel (dining room table), Alison Berger (handblown floor lamp), and Jean Prouvé, as well as custom pieces by Janson Goldstein (onyx table, dining room banquet). The collection of photography includes work by Richard Avedon, Sally Mann, and Uta Barth. A James Turrell hologram sits at the entry. Italian glasswork, African masks, an original Olivetti typewriter, and hand-sewn quilts are among the objects that enliven the space.

Floor Plan

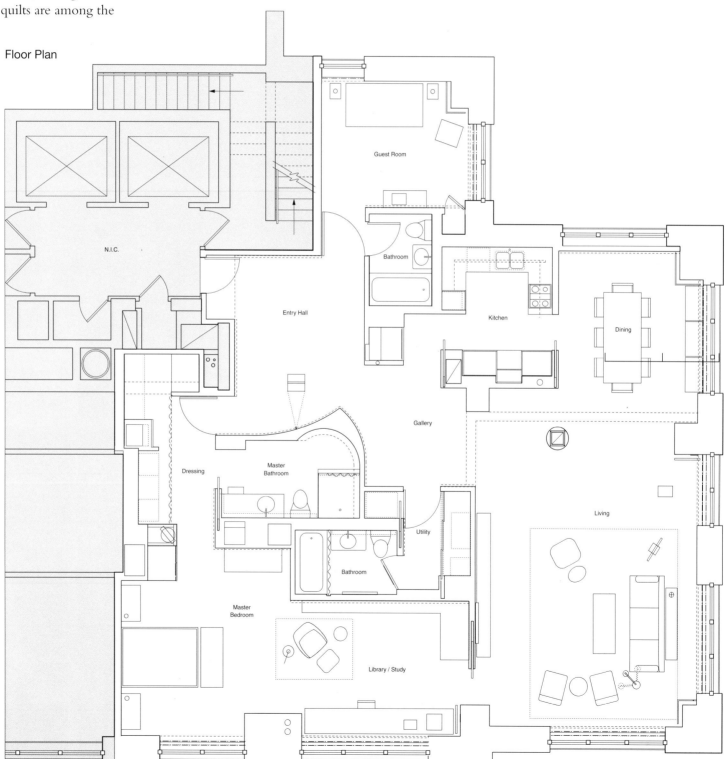

**RIGHT:** *View of living area from dining area*
**FOLLOWING PAGES:** *Dining area*

**THIS SPREAD:** *Master bedroom*

**ABOVE AND OPPOSITE:** *Master bathroom*

# Napolitano Residence

## ROBERT M. GURNEY, ARCHITECT

*Owner:* Ornella Napolitano
*Architect:* Robert M. Gurney, Architect, Washington, DC
*Design Team:* Robert M. Gurney and Hito Martinez (project designers)
*Engineer:* Tony Beale, Advance Engineers (structural)
*General Contractor:* M.T. Puskar Construction
*Interior Design:* Therese Baron Gurney
*Photography:* Hoachlander Davis Photography

*Location:* Washington, DC
*Program:* A total renovation of a ninteenth-century townhouse in a historic district. The new interior includes three bedrooms, three-and-one-half baths, living room, dining room, and kitchen.
*Square Footage:* 1900
*Mechanical System:* Heat pump, forced air
*Major Interior Materials:* Aluminum panels; anoline-dyed, maple, mahogany, and aluminum cabinetry; painted steel; perforated aluminum; black granite and green limestone countertops; black granite, green limestone, and Brazilian cherry floors
*Furnishings and Storage:* B&B Italia, Knoll Furniture, and Siam International
*Doors and Hardware:* Custom wood with FSB hardware, and custom steel with laminated glass and mahogany panels with Grant Hardware
*Fixtures:* Kohler and Franke
*Appliances and Equipment:* Bosch and KitchenAid

### Design

The existing interior of this row house was gutted and completely reworked. Planar walls and volumes organize, animate, and relate each room to the next. In the new scheme, the living room is relocated toward the rear of the house, away from the noise of the street. The new living room is naturally lit from the glass-paneled front door and indirectly from a linear skylight that filters light through a section of the second floor. A fireplace constructed of one-half-inch-thick aluminum panels, ash, and anoline-dyed boxes is set against mahogany panels and serves to anchor this space.

The new kitchen is inserted between the living and dining rooms and serves as a link between the two. Like the fireplace wall, the cabinetry is constructed of ash, mahogany, and aluminum. Here, these materials are set against black granite. An integral sliding panel between the dining room and the kitchen modulates views between these two spaces.

**RIGHT:** *Living room*

Existing Floor Plans

Building Section

Basement Floor Plan    First Floor Plan    Second Floor Plan

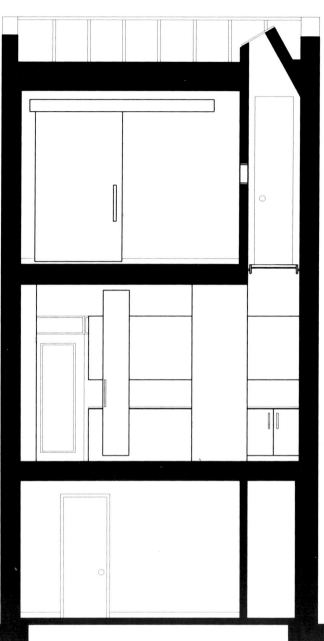

**OPPOSITE:** *Entry*

**RIGHT:** *Master bedroom*

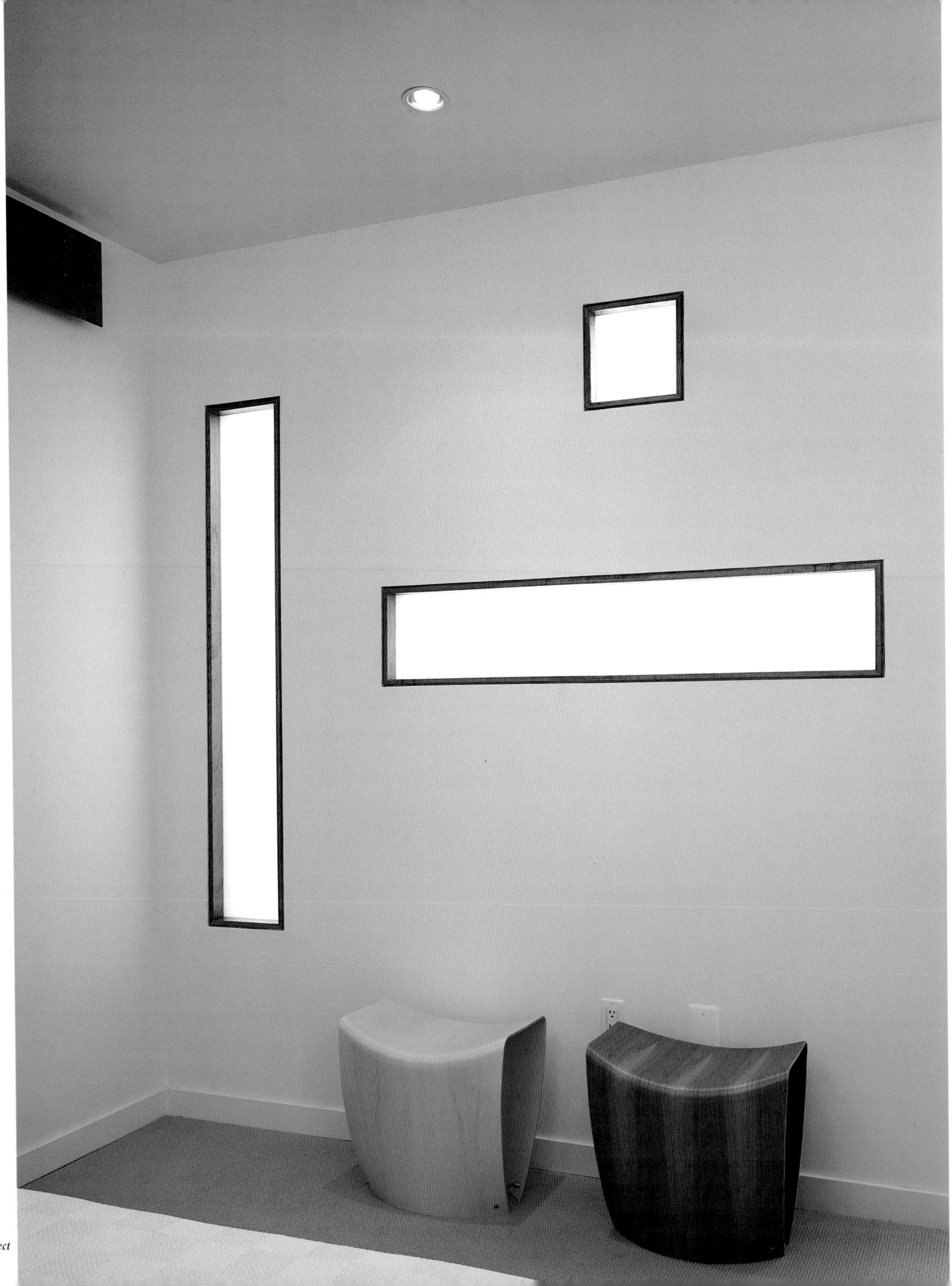

# Casa Dorado

## SOLIS BETANCOURT

*Owners:* Mr. and Mrs. Jorge Colon-Nevares
*Interior Design:* Solis Betancourt, Washington, DC
*Architect:* Ramirez De Arellano
*Engineer:* Arturo Diaz
*Landscape Architecture:* Gabriel Berriz and Associates
*General Contractor:* Raul Lopez
*Photography:* Gordon Beall

*Location:* Dorado Beach East, PR
*Program:* A weekend beach house and retreat for an adult family and grandchildren, with a vestibule, living room, den, two powder rooms, a kitchen, breakfast room, guest room, master suite, exterior terrace with exterior kitchen, laundry room, wine room, staff quarters, and three guest room suites, each with their own terrace
*Square Footage:* 7624
*Major Interior Materials:* Concrete (walls, ceilings) and travertine (floors)
*Doors and Hardware:* Distinctive Door Works (white oak doors) and Rocky Mountain Hardware
*Fixtures:* Newport Brass

### Design

The home is located on the golf course of the exclusive beach resort of Dorado, Puerto Rico. It was designed with the warm and quiet architectural references of the Spanish Colonial style. While certain architectural elements are traditional, the interior is a modern, tropical hacienda or country house. The home is sophisticated and timeless, with an emphasis on a fine collection of Puerto Rican paintings and sculpture.

Throughout the house, pigmented plaster-over-concrete walls create a neutral envelope for the dramatic artworks. The stone floors are neutral shades of travertine. Borders and baseboards are darker to mark the sequence of spaces in a classical manner.

The two-story-high living room is dramatic with several furniture groupings or arrangements to create a more intimate scale. There is also a long refractory-style table that can seat twelve for dinner.

Antique rough-hewn beams were used throughout the home to add warmth and texture and a sense of history.

**RIGHT:** *Sitting room*

**ABOVE AND OPPOSITE:** *Dining gallery*

**ABOVE:** *Master bathroom*
**LEFT:** *Master bedroom*

151

# New York City Apartment

ANDY GOLDSBOROUGH INTERIOR DESIGN

*Owners:* Withheld
*Interior Design:* Andy Goldsborough Interior Design,
New York, NY
*Photography:* Andrew French

*Location:* New York, NY
*Program:* Complete renovation of an existing apartment to
include a solarium, master bedroom, dining room, dining
alcove, kitchen, living room, and media room
*Square Footage:* 2000
*Major Interior Materials:* Plaster, glass door panels, and stain-
less steel
*Furnishings and Storage:* Knoll Studio, Old World Weavers,
Larsen, Cassina, Fred Silberman, Brunschwig & Fils, and
B&B Italia
*Fixtures:* Custom fixtures by Deborah Czeresko, MSK
Illuminations
*Appliances and Equipment:* Miele and Gaggenau

## Design

The client's desire for a minimalist environment
that would seamlessly blend the old details of the building with new modern furnishings and bold light fixtures drove the design of this apartment. The existing
floors were stained very dark to set off the fireplace and
traditional picture moldings and accentuate the ceiling
height. The apple-green Art Deco sofa in the living
room was inherited by the client and was the only
piece of existing furniture that was integrated into the
design. The challenge was to make the rest of the furnishings in the room very calm and neutral so as not to
visually compete with the sofa. The custom carpet,
based on a Chinese Art Deco design, incorporates the
sofa's color into the leaves of the carpet pattern, helping
to integrate the sofa into the room. Reflective surfaces
on the faceted drawer fronts of the 1940s Italian console
by Fontana Arte and the cast flowers in the Venini
chandelier cause the room to sparkle. The painting of
"Sprout" by Will Cotton looms above the one-of-a-
kind console and provides a sense of humor in an
otherwise very formal room. The monochromatic cool
blue-gray tones featured in the media alcove, which is
adjacent to the living room, provide a neutral backdrop
for watching movies and lounging.

Ascending the staircase, the floor color changes to a
bleached oak finish. The entire dining, kitchen, and
bedroom areas on the second floor are almost colorless,
further enhancing the floating quality of the apartment.
Custom carpets in the dining room and bedroom fade

**RIGHT:** *View through bedroom
etched-glass doors into the
solarium*

from charcoal gray to off-white, adding dimension to the floor surfaces. The existing roof of the apartment was replaced with glass, flooding the dining and kitchen areas with light.

Most of the horizontal planes and table surfaces on the second floor are glass, reflecting the sky and views. In the bedroom the doors to the solarium were custom made with acid-etched glass. Translucent window treatments in the bedroom and the solarium provide privacy but permit light to enter both rooms. The furnishings in the bedroom by modernist masters Poul Kjaerholm and Mies van der Rohe complement the 1940s Italian mirror by Fontana Arte. All of the ceiling fixtures on the second floor were custom made by artist Deborah Czeresko in varying degrees of clear and cloudy glass.

**RIGHT:** *Solarium detail*
**OPPOSITE:** *Dining room alcove*
**FOLLOWING PAGES:** *Dining and kitchen areas*

**PREVIOUS PAGES:** *View of living room and media room/den beyond*
**ABOVE:** *View of staircase to dining room and kitchen from living room*
**OPPOSITE, TOP:** *Living room*
**OPPOSITE, BOTTOM, AND LEFT:** *Living room details*

**LEFT:** *Master bedroom with solarium beyond*
**ABOVE:** *Fireplace in master bedroom*
**RIGHT:** *Master bedroom detail*

# Flatiron Loft

JANSON GOLDSTEIN

*Owner:* Withheld
*Interior Design:* Janson Goldstein, New York, NY
*Design Team:* Mark Janson and Hal Goldstein (partners)
and Christian Lynch (project architect)
*General Contractor:* On the Level
*Consultant:* Craig Roberts (lighting design)
*Photography:* Paul Warchol

*Location:* New York, NY
*Program:* An open loft for entertaining and displaying art
*Square Footage:* 2200
*Major Interior Materials:* Plaster (Art-in-Construction), mill-
work (Ino), and carpet (Beauvais)
*Furnishings and Storage:* Custom table by Janson Goldstein
*Fixtures:* Kroin and Grohe

## Design

This loft was designed as a showcase for entertaining and
for an extensive contemporary art collection. A series of
horizontal platforms and vertical planes expand and
contract the space, and thereby organize it. Service functions are located in the dark core of the building while
living, study, and sleeping functions are at the perimeter.
The entry/gallery space serves as a connector.

Color is used to bridge architecture with interior design.
Three colors, inspired by the paintings of Brice Marden,
establish the project palette, and serve to define the space
and add texture. The colors—chocolate brown, blue-
gray, and black-blue—appear first as integral color plaster
planes that delineate the entry/gallery space and the liv-
ing/study space, which are at opposite ends of the loft.
All other materials and textures are derivative of these
three surfaces. The floor serves as the palette's connect-
ing element, where the warmth of oak is allowed to
penetrate a blue-gray stain, fusing the three colors of the
palette in one surface. The floor appears blue adjacent to
the brown plaster wall and brown adjacent to the blue-
gray wall. To serve as a neutral background, all other
walls and ceilings are white.

A series of gray, brown, and blue variations of cloth and
leather are used on sofas and chairs. Custom-designed
tables utilize dyed ash, creating a brown-black combination. Individual groupings of furniture were conceived as
three-dimensional paintings.

The art collection is arranged to encourage one's
movement through the space—asymmetrical placement

**RIGHT:** *View of dining area from living area*

ADAM FUSS

JAPANESE ART AFTER 1945

leads the eye from one art work to the next. The composition is designed to be integral with the articulation of the space, and the lighting is designed to enhance this relationship.

**RIGHT:** *Entry*
**OPPOSITE:** *Living area*

**ABOVE:** *Dining area*
**LEFT:** *Kitchen*

# Capitol Apartment

## McINTURFF ARCHITECTS

*Owner:* Withheld
*Architect:* McInturff Architects, Bethesda, MD
*Design Team:* Mark McInturff (principal)and Christopher Boyd (design associate)
*Photography:* Julia Heine

*Location:* Washington, DC
*Program:* Renovation of an existing apartment to include a living room, dining room, kitchen, master suite with dressing area, bath, office, and guest suite with bath
*Square Footage:* 1788
*Major Interior Materials:* Venetian plaster (Warnock Studios) and stucco (Jamie Zimmet)
*Furnishings and Storage:* Custom wooden built-ins, panels, and trim (A. E. Boland), Knoll, and owner's vintage mid-century furniture
*Fixtures:* Porcher, Kohler, and Dornbracht
*Appliances and Equipment:* Miele, Dacor, Sub-Zero, and Dornbracht

### Design

This project centered on combining three very small apartments in a 1960s building into one apartment with far more generous rooms. The result is a flexible open plan that takes advantage of the sixty-five-feet-high window wall overlooking an urban park. All major rooms in the apartment are placed along this wall, while the kitchen, bathrooms, and closets are tucked in the windowless spaces behind them. Walls dressed in two colors of venetian plaster, along with a black marble slab, define the boundaries of the living areas. Other walls are thick, sculpted natural stucco.

The crisp, modern space is a perfect complement to the client's collection of vintage mid-century furniture, which includes a Bertoia Bird chair and a Tulip chair by Saarinen. These pieces are augmented by reproductions of famous designs of the era, including an Eames lounge chair and ottoman, as well as Bertoia bar stools, a Saarinen coffee table, and Walter Knoll lounge chairs by Knoll Furniture.

A richly stained and polished wooden floor serves as a unifying element throughout the apartment. Carefully crafted wooden built-ins, panels, and trim echo the equally fine craftsmanship of the mid-century furnishings.

**RIGHT:** *Living room*

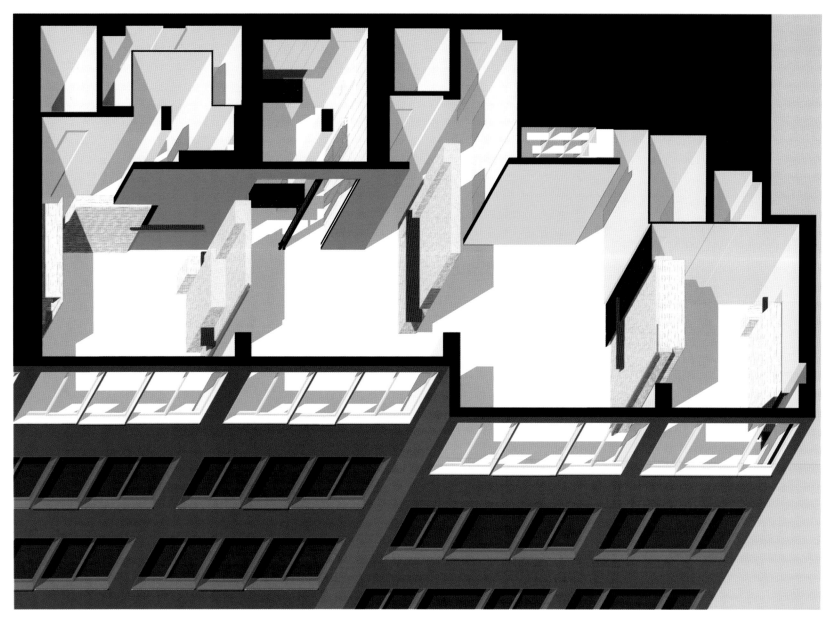

**ABOVE:** *Computer model*
**RIGHT:** *View of living room and dining room beyond*

**ABOVE:** *Dining room with doors to kitchen open*
**LEFT:** *Latch detail of sliding kitchen doors*
**OPPOSITE:** *View of kitchen from dining room with sliding doors in open position*

**ABOVE:** *Kitchen*
**OPPOSITE:** *Bedroom detail*

# Fauntleroy Residence

## SUYAMA PETERSON DEGUCHI

*Owner:* Withheld
*Architect:* Suyama Peterson Deguchi, Seattle, WA
*Design Team:* George Suyama (principal), David Derrer, Chris Haddad, Carl Mahaney, Kevin Miyamura, Matt Scholl, and Jeff King
*Engineer:* Swenson Say Faget (structural)
*General Contractor:* Crocker Construction
*Consultants:* Alchemie (landscape), Brian Hood (lighting design), and Geotech (geotechnical)
*Photography:* Paul Warchol

*Location:* Seattle, WA
*Program:* Multipurpose main room, which includes living and dining areas, a master bedroom and bath, study/media/office, lower bath, utility room, wine room, outdoor living and dining, and a garage
*Square Footage:* 2600
*Structural System:* Fir stick-frame with exposed three-by-ten-feet rafters
*Major Exterior Materials:* Western red cedar siding, zinc roof, and veneer stucco over hardy panels
*Major Interior Materials:* Veneer plaster walls, concrete floors, plywood ceilings, and MDF cabinets
*Doors and Hardware:* Fleetwood aluminum sliders, Corbin hardware solid-core painted doors, and Soss and custom pivot-hinges
*Windows:* Custom VG fir windows with aluminum stops
*Fixtures:* Vola, Toto, Zuma, and Elkay
*Appliances and Equipment:* Gaggenau, GE, and Fisher & Paykel

## Design

The site is a narrow beachfront lot with three existing structures, one modest main house and two rustic cabins. The panoramic views to Puget Sound and the mountains are framed by four elegant fir trees planted by the original owner.

The beachfront community in which the house is located was developed at the turn of the last century as a summer getaway. Over the years many of the cabins have been replaced with larger permanent homes, and few remnants of the old community remain.

This house was designed as a minimalist counterpoint to protect and preserve the fragile nature of two existing rustic cabins that remain on the site. On approach from the street, the house appears as a simple one-story structure, which subtly references its older neighbors. Once through the entry gate, however, the dramatic expanse of the simple shed roof becomes apparent, drawing attention to the view of sound and mountains beyond.

**RIGHT:** *Den and study*

The house is a series of sequential spaces. Exterior courtyards and interior spaces weave together and constantly blur the relationship between outside and inside. Reflecting pools are used to reference and recall the distant views of water.

The entry terrace, which serves as an outdoor sitting room, was placed at the east end of the house away from the water view to provide protection from the prevailing winds off the water. A fireplace provides heat for year-round usage. The house is built around an open plan with simple, large gestures. The master bedroom is lowered four feet, allowing uninterrupted views from the main space and reinforcing the notion of a picnic shelter. All details were conceived to eliminate as much visual clutter as possible and add further contrast with the existing cabins.

Second Floor Plan

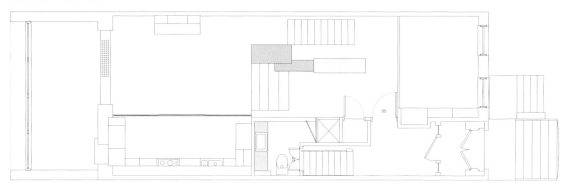

First Floor Plan

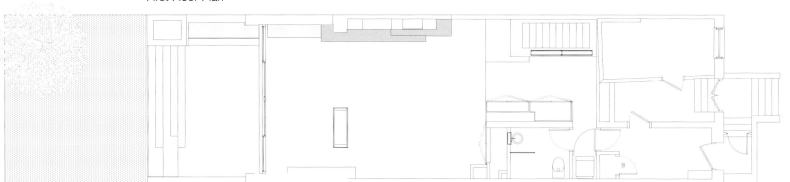

**LEFT:** *Rear facade with door to den*
**OPPOSITE:** *Outdoor living and dining areas with main entrance to house beyond*

**OPPOSITE:** *View from pool to outdoor living and dining areas*
**LEFT:** *Outdoor living area*
**BELOW:** *View of deck and outdoor living area*

**ABOVE:** *Living/dining and kitchen areas*
**OPPOSITE:** *Corridor to wine cellar*

**ABOVE:** *Exterior pond view*
**OPPOSITE:** *View from kitchen*

# Siegel Residence

## BUSH INTERIORS

*Owner:* Greg Siegel
*Interior Design:* Bush Interiors, Marina Del Rey, CA
*Engineer:* Gordon Polon Engineers
*General Contractor:* D.A. Foster and Associates
*Photography:* Grey Crawford

*Location:* Los Angeles, CA
*Program:* Renovation of a mid-century modern home to include an entry, lounge, living room, dining room, open kitchen, guest bedroom and bath, office, master bedroom and bath suite, garage, and pool patio
*Square Footage:* 2000
*Major Exterior Materials:* Plaster and glass
*Major Interior Materials:* Terrazzo, walnut, high-gloss lacquers, stainless steel, and limestone
*Furnishings and Storage:* Infinite Designs
*Doors and Hardware:* D-Line
*Appliances and Equipment:* Jenn-Air, Dacor, Thermador, and Fisher & Paykel

### Design

The redesign of this mid-century home in the Hollywood Hills area was driven by the owner's wish to create a clean, modern environment that would be minimal, masculine, and stylish. The goal was to open up the main public rooms to create one large open living area. The existing white terrazzo floors visually linked the kitchen, dining room, living room, lounge, and entry. Pale tones of white, sand, and sky blue were introduced to create a light but varied base palette. Dark walnut elements were then added to provide depth, character, and contrast. This palette was intentionally reserved to provide a neutral foundation for the striking modern red sculpture that is the focal point of the interior.

The abstract forms of the dining set and coffee table were custom designed by Bush Interiors and Silho Furniture. These pieces anchor the main living space. A pendant light fixture marks the position of each piece from above. The forms of the light fixtures by Le Klimt are repeated in a concrete-disc wall sculpture and more subtly in the porthole windows in the doors.

The palette of the master bedroom is a subtle study of white and walnut on sand. The bedroom walls are covered with grass cloth; the master bathroom is concealed by pivoting and sliding shoji screens. A large, custom platform bed is the focus and backdrop of the bedroom and gives the impression of a larger space.

**RIGHT:** *Living area*

**RIGHT:** *Entry*
**OPPOSITE:** *View of dining area
and abstract sculpture from living
area*

Floor Plan

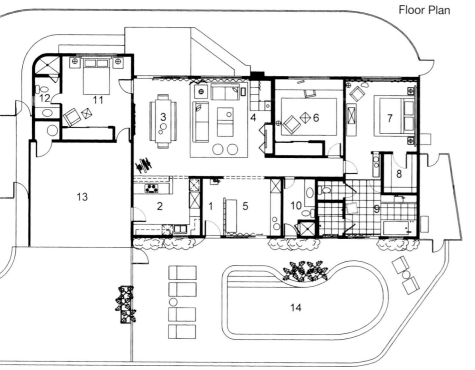

1. Entry
2. Kitchen
3. Dining
4. Living
5. Lounge
6. Office
7. Master Bedroom
8. Closet
9. Master Bathroom
10. Bathroom
11. Guest Bedroom
12. Guest Bathroom
13. Garage
14. Pool Patio

**ABOVE:** *View of dining area from living area*
**OPPOSITE:** *Dining area with custom-made table by interior designer*

ABOVE: *Kitchen*
LEFT: *Master bathroom*

**ABOVE, LEFT:** *View from master bedroom*
**ABOVE, RIGHT:** *Detail of platform bed in master bedroom*

# Smith Apartment

## ROBERT M. GURNEY, ARCHITECT

*Owner:* David Smith
*Architect:* Robert M. Gurney, Architect, Washington, DC
*Design Team:* Robert M. Gurney and Claire Larsen Andreas
(project architect)
*General Contractor:* M.T. Puskar Construction
*Interior Design:* Therese Baron Gurney
*Photography:* Maxwell Mackenzie Photography

*Location:* Washington, DC
*Program:* A total renovation of an early-twentieth-century
apartment integrating art, architecture, and furnishings within
an open floor plan that includes a living/dining area, kitchen,
master bedroom, guest bedroom, and two bathrooms
*Square Footage:* 1900
*Mechanical System:* Heat pump, forced air
*Major Interior Materials:* Disc-grinded aluminum, steel
(painted and disc-grinded), anoline-dyed maple, mahogany,
and stainless steel cabinetry, stainless steel backsplash, blue
pearl-granite and green limestone countertops, and
Brazilian cherry floors
*Furnishings and Storage:* B&B Italia, McMurray Contract
Furniture, Knoll, Brueton International, Herman Miller, Flos,
Room & Board, and custom pieces by designer
*Fixtures:* Kohler, Porcher, and Franke
*Appliances and Equipment:* Sub-Zero, Miele, Bosch, and
KitchenAid

### Design

The existing apartment in a Beaux-Arts inspired building was arranged as a series of narrow compartmental-
ized rooms. To liberate the space, the interior was
stripped to its essential structure and infrastructure. A
series of steel columns, chasiss, and plumbing stacks
imposed a number of constraints. Although the existing
unit has three exposures, the major south-facing wall
opens to a large hotel that is relatively close and unin-
spired. For this reason, the architect designed a residence
that turns inward.

The new scheme is organized around a curved wall
intended to juxtapose the orthogonal column grid. This
is reinforced at the entry with a system of sliding glass
panels on an axis to the radial point. The open plan is
infused with a contemporary palette of richly textured
and colored materials that produce a refined, highly
detailed urban space. Ceiling heights vary throughout
the apartment to accommodate new mechanical systems
and infrastructure. This variation is most evident in the
rotated ellipse located in the ceiling above the central
living area.

**RIGHT:** *Living area*

Existing Floor Plan

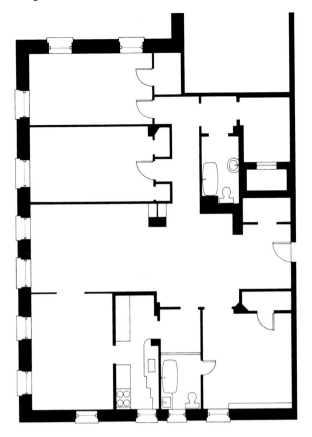

Axonometric

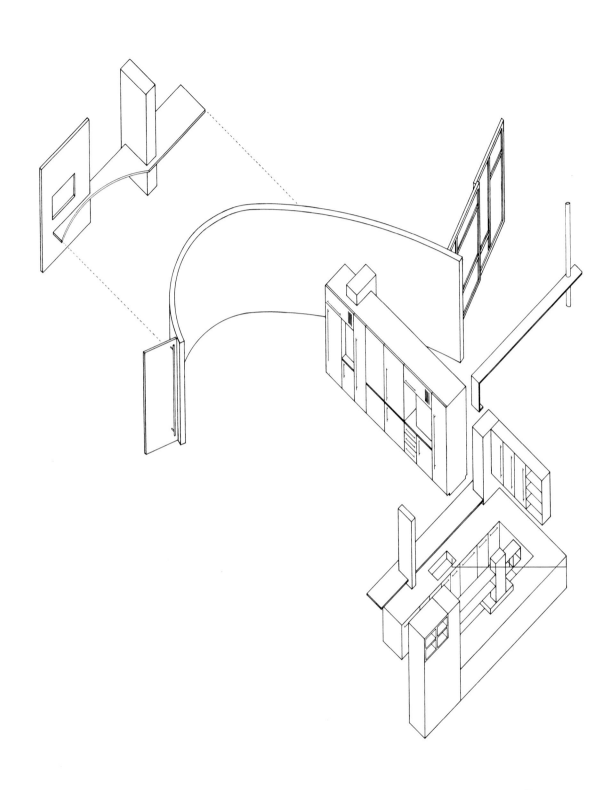

Floor Plan

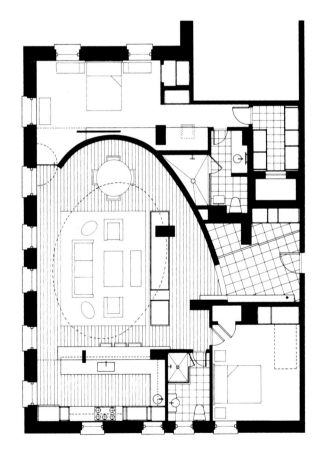

**OPPOSITE:** *Entry*

**OPPOSITE:** *View of living area from open kitchen*
**ABOVE:** *Kitchen*

ABOVE AND OPPOSITE: *Master bedroom*

# Vertical House

## LORCAN O'HERLIHY ARCHITECTS

*Owners:* Lorcan O'Herlihy and Cornelia Hayes O'Herlihy
*Architect:* Lorcan O'Herlihy Architects, Culver City, CA
*Design Team:* Lorcan O'Herlihy (principal), David Thompson and Kuo-Huei Tsai (project managers), Michael Poirier and Hillary Leonard (project team)
*Engineer:* Paul Franceschi
*General Contractor:* Above Board Construction
*Photography:* Michael Weschler

*Location:* Venice, CA
*Program:* A single-family residence with living, dining, and kitchen areas, a master suite, two guest bedrooms, three-and-one-half bathrooms, and a roof deck
*Square Footage:* 2300
*Structural System:* Steel-moment frame with metal-stud curtain wall
*Mechanical System:* Gas-fired forced air
*Major Exterior Materials:* Painted cement board and glass
*Doors and Hardware:* Painted sliders with Haefele hardware
*Windows:* Aluminum, Profilit channel glass
*Fixtures:* Dornbracht, Duravit, and Hans Grohe
*Appliances and Equipment:* Frigidaire

### Design

Sited on a tight lot in increasingly architecturally-hip Venice, California, this house, designed for the architect and his family, pulls out all the stops to take advantage of every asset available, from light to views. The exterior is an innovative use of vertical strips of cement board painted black interspersed with three types of vertical glazing. While appearing randomly placed, the glazing, which is clear, translucent, and frosted, is in fact very carefully placed to manipulate limited views and light while screening views of neighboring houses immediately adjacent. The hybrid nature of the surface formalizes the expression of this simple box while responding to the site restrictions. Verticality is expressed in the central stair core, which extends beyond the roof for views of the Pacific Ocean, which is only three blocks from the site.

To maximize usable square footage, the site restrictions have been pushed to the limit in both plan and elevation, forcing the linearity of the design on paper to be translated in built form. The steel-moment frame frees the skin from structural constraints, allowing an unrestricted rhythm of glazing, channel glass, and solid panels. This exterior structural support system also frees the interior from structural constraints, allowing for a free-flowing, open-space design.

To capture the views, the living room and kitchen are on the third floor and a small, glass-enclosed room is placed on the roof. The bedrooms are on the second floor, and a small studio and parking area are on the ground level. Most of the furniture and cabinetry were designed by the architect to blend seamlessly with the dramatic yet pragmatic architecture.

**RIGHT:** *Living area*

**Third Floor Plan**

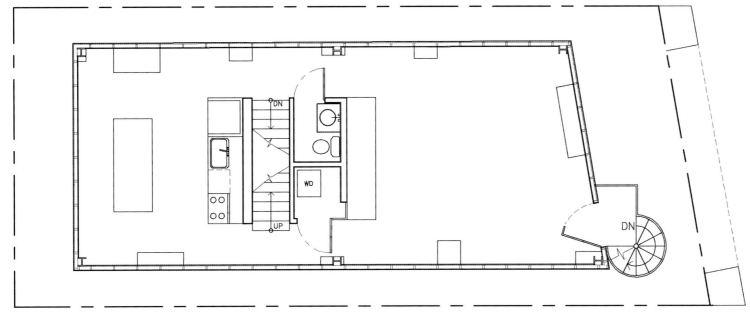

**Second Floor Plan**

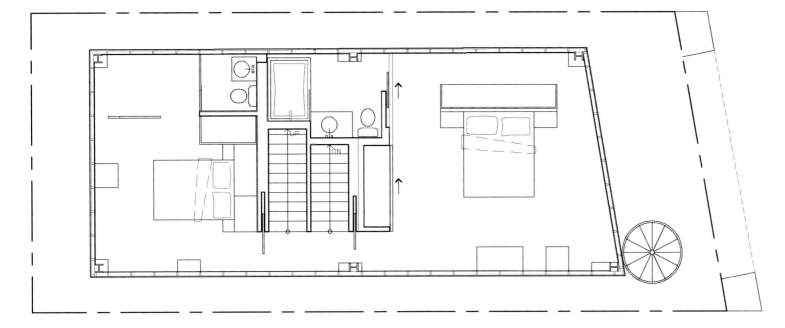

**Ground Floor Plan**

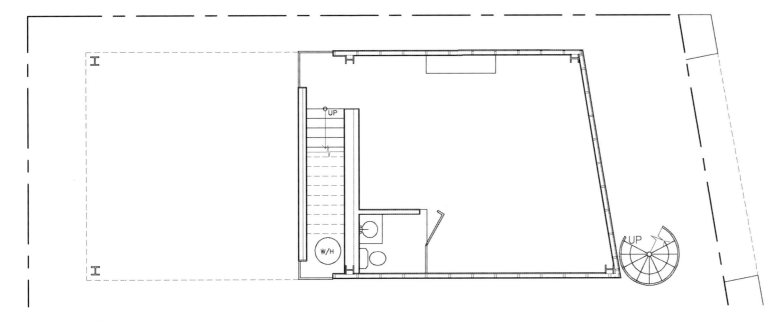

Computer Models

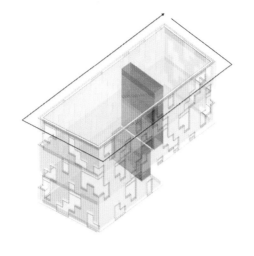

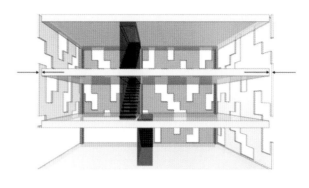

Floor Plans

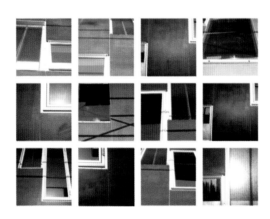

[Carport]　　[Bedroom 1]

[Ground Floor Plan]

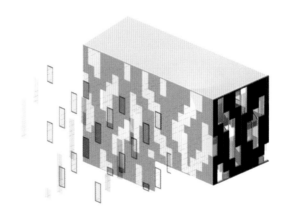

[Bedroom 2]　　[Master Bedroom]

[Second Floor Plan]

Conceptual Models

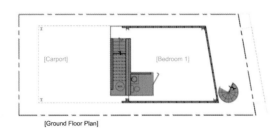

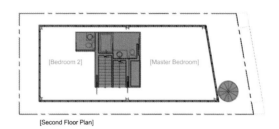

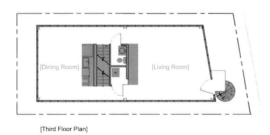

[Dining Room]　　[Living Room]

[Third Floor Plan]

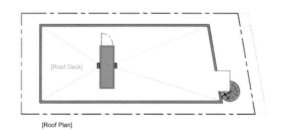

[Roof Deck]

[Roof Plan]

**OPPOSITE:** *Street-side elevation*
**ABOVE:** *Vertical windows at dusk*
**RIGHT:** *Exterior circular stairway*

**OPPOSITE AND ABOVE:** *Third-floor living area*

**OPPOSITE:** *Living room cabinetry*
**ABOVE:** *Master bedroom cabinetry*

**LEFT:** *Master bedroom*
**ABOVE:** *Master bathroom detail*

# Riverside Drive Apartment

JANSON GOLDSTEIN

*Owner:* Withheld
*Interior Design:* Janson Goldstein, New York, NY
*Design Team:* Mark Janson and Hal Goldstein (principals) and Takaaki Kawabata (project architect)
*Engineer:* Tri-Power Engineering
*General Contractor:* On the Level
*Consultants:* Bill Jansing (lighting), Aytan Diamond (mill-work), and K. Flam Associates (upholstery fabrication)
*Photography:* Paul Warchol

*Location:* New York, NY
*Program:* The renovation of an existing prewar apartment that includes a living room, dining room, kitchen, master suite, guest room, and home office
*Square Footage:* 2000
*Major Interior Materials:* Plaster (Art-in-Construction), lime-stone (Stone Source)
*Furnishings and Storage:* Custom walnut bed by Janson Goldstein

## Design

Retention of the building's early-twentieth-century character was a priority for this apartment. An expansive loft space was not the goal. Rather, the owners wanted a home that would blend openness and intimacy and allow them to express their love of fine arts, books, and music. A color palette was developed from the Agnes Martin painting located at the entry. Fabrics such as suede, cottons, and linens were chosen for their texture and luxurious qualities.

At the center of the apartment a glowing "lantern" provides warm and ambient light. It is made from fabric panels and incandescent lights that are recessed in the walls. The light source is hidden as well as the frame that supports the fabric. The "lantern" is best viewed in the living room from the suede-covered Barcelona chairs.

The master suite features a custom walnut bed designed by Janson Goldstein and hanging fabric panels that serve as window treatments. The cool blue-green panels fill the room with ambient color as natural light is filtered through them. The bathroom features a limestone floor with a sandblasted slab for the floor of the shower. The slab ends in a hidden trough where the water runs off.

**RIGHT:** *Living area*

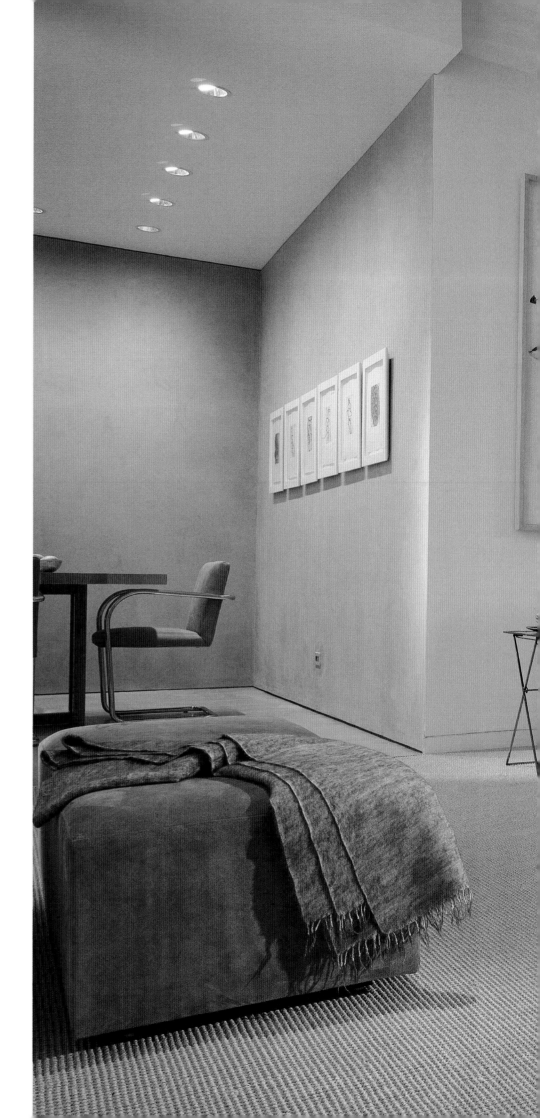

Floor Plan

Master Bedroom

Master Bathroom

Bathroom

Study

Living Room

Kitchen

Entry

Bath

Guest Room

**RIGHT:** *View of lantern from living area*

**LEFT AND ABOVE, RIGHT:** *Dining area*
**RIGHT:** *Kitchen*

**OPPOSITE:** *Master bedroom*
**ABOVE:** *Master bathroom*

# Tribeca Apartment

TOCAR, INC.

*Owner:* Withheld
*Interior Design:* Tocar, Inc., New York, NY
*Design Team:* Susan Bednar and Christina Sulivan
*General Contractor:* Fortuny Interiors
*Photography:* Mark Lins, Tocar

*Location:* New York, NY
*Program:* Renovation of an old spice-factory loft to include a master bedroom, living room, kitchen, and dining room
*Square Footage:* 2370
*Major Interior Materials:* Restored brick walls, rough-hewn wood beams, cherry oak, walnut, cast iron, and stone
*Furnishings and Storage:* Poggenpol cherry cabinetry, custom furniture by Tocar, Inc.
*Fixtures:* Tolomeo and Costanza
*Appliances and Equipment:* Viking

## Design

This renovated apartment is located in a former spice factory built in 1859. The interior design employs a combination of modern and traditional furnishings using rich woods, muted colors, and fine fabrics that complement the original architecture of the building. The free-form public space celebrates the idea of a loft space with the main entertaining spaces—the kitchen bar area, the living area, and the dining area—flowing one unto the other.

The designers took their cues from the existing space and combined the colors of the original brick, wood beams, and painted steel beams into the furniture and fabrics, using deep red silk and taupe-brown accents. To keep the primary focus on the architecture they floated the living and dining seating areas off the walls. This also serves to highlight the loft's generous expanse of windows and to create a free-flowing seating arrangement for entertaining.

To give the master bedroom a sense of serenity, the designers created a spa environment with light furnishings and soft blue decorative accents. The brick walls were painted a Montgomery white and stark white wood blinds were added to the large windows to maximize the space. Decorative accents such as the Vernrr Panton lucite box and blue-and-white Chinese jars were added for a perfect balance between modern and traditional styles.

**RIGHT:** *Living room*

**ABOVE:** *Master bedroom*
**OPPOSITE:** *Dining room*

# Zeno Residence

BUSH INTERIORS

*Owners:* Jamie Bush and Stephen Calipari
*Interior Design:* Bush Interiors, Marina Del Rey, CA
*Engineer:* Gordon Polon Engineers
*General Contractor:* Lorenzo Medina
*Photography:* Grey Crawford

*Location:* Venice, CA
*Program:* This duplex consists of an entry, lounge, living room, dining room, open kitchen, guest bedroom and bath, master bedroom and bath, garage, pool, and patio
*Square Footage:* 2000
*Major Interior Materials:* Calcutta-gold marble tile, high-gloss lacquers, mosaic tile, vintage wallpapers, and limed white oak
*Furnishings and Storage:* Interior Resources and IKEA
*Appliances and Equipment:* GE Profile, Kenmore, and Bosch

## Design

The duplex was created for the designer's partner and himself to live in one half and a relative to live in the other half. The center portion would be used as a piano studio for teaching. A compound approach was taken for this small lot to maximize the exterior spaces while maintaining privacy in this urban neighborhood. Tall white gates and hedges surround the property, allowing interior spaces to open up to the patios and the deck.

The home is divided into two zones: the studio area finished in woods and beige and yellow tones, and the living areas finished in white marble and hot colors. The studio and the adjacent waiting room are identical spaces with a modern Asian influence. Limed oak flooring and walls rise to caps of graphic wallpapered ceilings. The vintage Capi shell chandeliers by Verner Panton add a natural decadence to the spaces as do the German ceramic sconces on the walls.

The living areas are a mix of modern detailing coupled with Hollywood Regency furnishings. Built-in white lacquered cabinetry, floor-to-ceiling walls of tile, and mid-century lighting create a clean neutral base. Colorful Regency side chairs, mirrored sunburst screens, and lotus flower pendant fixtures provide a certain shocking glamour to the modern backdrop.

Several visual tricks were utilized to give the perception of a larger more spacious home. Interior and exterior rooms were reorganized so door openings would align and provide views through multiple rooms. These openings received pairs of narrow doors, which made the eight-foot ceilings appear taller. Marble floor tiles were laid throughout the house and onto the patios to create a continuous modern texture.

**RIGHT:** *Living room*

First Floor Plan

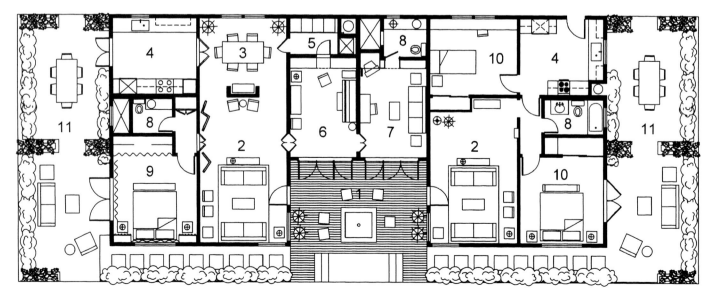

1. Front Deck
2. Living
3. Dining
4. Kitchen
5. Pantry
6. Studio
7. Den
8. Bathroom
9. Master Bedroom
10. Bedroom
11. Back Patio

1. Front Deck

**THIS PAGE:** *Piano studio and waiting room*
**OPPOSITE:** *Entry*

East 100th Street BRUCE DAVIDSON

ROSS BLECKNER

**ABOVE:** *Kitchen with view to patio*
**OPPOSITE:** *Living room detail*

# Index